Baby Kangaroo Facts for Kids and Adults

Informative Guide on Australian Kangaroos

How baby born, joey, pouch, feeding, Red Kangaroo, Eastern Grey, as Pets

By Les O. Tekcard

Copyright © February 2014 Baby Kangaroo Facts For Kids and Adults by Les O. Tekcard
All rights reserved. No part of this publication may be reproduced, distributed, or transmitted in any form or by any means, including photocopying, recording, or other electronic or mechanical methods, without the prior written permission of the publisher, except in the case of brief quotations embodied in critical reviews and certain other non commercial uses permitted by copyright law. For permission requests, please write to the publisher.

ISBN : 978-0-9923922-1-5

Printed in Australia

Disclaimer
Although the author and publisher have made every effort to ensure that the information in this book was correct at press time, the author and publisher do not assume and hereby disclaim any liability to any party for any loss, injury, damage, or disruption caused by errors or omissions, whether such errors or omissions result from negligence, accident, non functional websites, or any other cause. Any advice or strategy contains herein, may not be suitable for every individual.

Foreword

In the 1967 version of "Dr. Doolittle," actor Rex Harrison sang of his desire to "Talk to the Animals," saying:

"I would converse in polar bear, python, and I would curse in fluent kangaroo. If people ask me, 'can you speak rhinocerous?' I'd say, 'of courserous!' Can't you?'"

I'll leave it to you to decide if kangaroos curse, but for the most part, I regard them as much more placid animals. Left to their own devices, roos don't ask all that much of the world – some shade, a place to graze, the freedom to be what they are.

That last is always the sticking point with me on the subject of exotic animals kept in companionship with humans.

Let me be quick to say that roos can be excellent companions. Especially when they have been hand reared, these remarkable marsupials are capable of great love for and loyalty to human beings.

The real issue of their suitability as companion animals rests more on us than on the kangaroos themselves. I heartily encourage an active interest in all the macropods – wallabies, wallaroos kangaroos – and in the broader world of marsupials.

Who isn't beguiled by the life of a baby – a joey – that begins securely snuggled in its mother's pouch? But what is even more wondrous is the first journey that joey makes.

Foreword

It emerges from the womb no larger than a bean and follows a path the mother kangaroo has licked into her fur. The tiny little joey, then properly called a neonate, makes its way up and into the pouch and onto one of its mother's life-sustaining nipples.

Over the next few weeks to months that tiny creatures becomes a miniature copy of the adult kangaroo, progressing to peering over the edge of the pouch and then one day making its first exploratory leap into the world.

Baby animals of all kinds are adorable and beguiling, but joeys have an alert charm all their own. They are boisterous and inquisitive while also being cuddly and adorable. Falling in love with one is so simple it's done before you get the first "aw" out of your mouth.

If, however, you want to make a kangaroo a part of your life, you have to consider that the adorable little joey will one day be a full grown adult of likely 5 feet / 1.5 meters or more in stature.

A kangaroo is not a house pet, and is, in fact, more akin to keeping livestock than any other analogy I can offer. Roos eat hay, mixed foods, and horse pellets or "cake."

They live outside in fenced pens, and they need pastures to run, roam, and graze.

Foreword

If you cannot provide these things, you should not have a kangaroo. It really is just that simple, for your own good and for the good of the animal.

In this book, I will attempt to give you as much information as possible about raising a joey and living with a full grown kangaroo. Only you can decide the best course of action in regard to bringing a roo into your life.

If you are afforded the correct circumstances, life with a kangaroo will be an adventure for upwards to 20 years. It will be the ride – or the hop – of a lifetime.

Even the most experienced and dedicated kangaroo owners will readily admit these are not easy animals to keep, but they are worth it. Read on to find out why.

Acknowledgments

I would like to extend my sincerest thanks to my friends and family who supported me throughout this journey. I'd like to thank my wife, especially, for her endless love understanding and accompanying me on some of my long trips in the Australian outback.

Acknowledgments

Table of Contents

Foreword 1

Acknowledgments 5

Table of Contents 7

Chapter 1 – The World of Marsupials 13

    1.) Marsupial Reproduction 14

    2.) The Macropod Marsupials 14

        a.) Red Kangaroo 17

        b.) Eastern Grey Kangaroo 18

        c.) Western Grey Kangaroo 18

        d.) Antilopine Kangaroo 19

    3.) Physical Characteristics of Macropods 20

        a.) The Mechanics of Hopping 21

        b.) Grazing Herbivores 23

Chapter 2 – Kangaroos in the Wild 25

    1.) Potential Aggression 26

    2.) Handling Aggressive Behavior 27

    3.) Watch, Don't Interact 28

Chapter 3 – What to Know Before Buying 31

    1.) Do I Need a License? 31

        a.) Laws in the U.S. 32

        b.) Licensing in the U.K. 34

Table of Contents

2.) Keeping Multiple Kangaroos? 36

3.) Kangaroos and Other Pets? 36

4.) Cost of Care 37

    a.) Initial Costs 37

    b.) Monthly Expenses 39

5.) Buying in the U.S. 41

6.) Buying in the U.K. 42

7.) Buying a Healthy Kangaroo 43

Pros and Cons of Owning a Kangaroo 44

Chapter 4 – Keeping Kangaroos as Pets 45

1.) A Joey's First Year 45

    a.) Milk Replacers 46

    b.) A Substitute Pouch 47

    c.) Maintaining the Correct Temperature 48

    d.) Feeding Your Joey 49

    e.) Toileting 50

    f.) Weaning 50

    g.) Playpens 51

2.) Becoming an Adult 51

    a.) Types of Food 52

    b.) Dispensing Food 53

3.) Outside Enclosure Requirements 54

Table of Contents

- a.) Fencing 54
- b.) Holding Area 55
- c.) Shelters 56
- d.) Furnishings 56
- 4.) Suggested Maintenance 57

Chapter 5 – Kangaroo Reproduction 59
- 1.) Kangaroo Breeding 60
  - a.) Fertility 60
- 2.) Mating and Birth 61
- 3.) Journey to the Pouch 62
- 4.) In the Pouch 63
- 5.) Pouch Life Ends 64

Chapter 6 – Hand Rearing a Joey 67
- 1.) Rescued Joeys 67
  - a.) A Word on Handling 68
- 2.) A Substitute Pouch 68
- 3.) Regulating Temperature 69
- 4.) Diet and Nutrition 70
- 5.) Selecting a Teat 71

Chapter 7 – Kangaroo Health 73
- 1.) Common Health Problems 73
  - a.) Hair Loss 74

Table of Contents

- b.) Flea Infestations 74
- c.) Ticks 75
- d.) Prolapsed Bowel 75
- e.) Scours or Diarrhea 76
- f.) Thrush 76
- g.) Pneumonia 77
- h.) Necrobacillosis (Lumpy Jaw) 77
- 2.) Dealing with Injuries 78
- 3.) Administering First Aid 80
  - a.) Clear the Airway 81
  - b.) Stop the Bleeding 81
  - c.) Maintain Body Temperature 82
  - d.) Minimize Stress 82

Chapter 8 – Roo Human Interest Stories 85
- 1.) Oklahoma Women Moves into the Zoo 85
- 2.) HOA Objects to Mike the Kangaroo 88
- 3.) Queensland Man Advocates for Roo Lovers 89
- 4.) Kangaroo Rescue and Rehab in the U.S. 91

Kid Talk: Understanding the Kangaroo's World 93
- A World of Marsupials 93
- Kangaroos, The Biggest Marsupial 94
- Keep Your Distance from Wild Kangaroos 95

Table of Contents

Big Kangaroos Start Out Really Small 97

Hopping to Get Along 99

Do They Box? 100

Can They Be Tame? 100

Afterword 103

Frequently Asked Questions 107

Relevant Websites 113

Glossary 117

Index 121

Chapter 1 – The World of Marsupials

The most distinctive characteristic of marsupials, and the one that most people already know, is that these wonderfully unique creatures carry their young, called "joeys," in a pouch or "marsupium."

The period of time a baby spends in the pouch varies by species from 120 to 400 days. During that time, it's a common and adorable sight to see the little joey poke its head up to have a look around or to hop in and out of its "room" in between outings.

The world of marsupials includes some fascinating and well-loved animals including kangaroos, wombats, wallabies, koalas, opossums, and even the Tasmanian devil.

Chapter 1 – The World of Marsupials

There are 334 existing species of marsupials in the world. About 100 of those are found in the Americas, but only one, the opossum, lives in North America.

Seventy percent of the world's marsupials reside in Australia and New Guinea, as well as on the adjacent islands.

1.) Marsupial Reproduction

In most mammals, babies develop inside the mother's womb in a placenta until they are ready to be born. This doesn't happen with marsupials.

Marsupial babies stay inside their mother's womb for just 4-5 weeks. When the joey is born it is roughly the size of a bean and is properly described as a "neonate."

This defenseless creature literally faces an uphill climb at birth. The tiny joey must make its way up the mother's body along a trail she has licked for it to follow in her fur.

Once the neonate is inside the pouch, it attaches itself to one of its mother's teats or nipples from which it will draw nourishment throughout the remainder of its development.

2.) The Macropod Marsupials

Kangaroos are the best known of the world's marsupials, and an unofficial symbol of Australia. Their iconic profile can be seen on all kinds of signage in popular culture, on

Chapter 1 – The World of Marsupials

the national coat of arms, and even on some denominations of currency.

Kangaroos belong to the family *Macropodidae*, which translates from the Latin to "large foot." There are 40 species in this group of marsupials. The smaller members are the wallabies, while the largest, *Macropos rufus*, the Red Kangaroo, stands as tall as a man.

Chapter 1 – The World of Marsupials

The four species of kangaroos are:

- Red Kangaroo (*Macropus rufus*)
- Eastern Grey Kangaroo (*Macropus giganteus*)
- Western Grey Kangaroo (*Macropus fuliginosus*)
- Antilopine Kangaroo (*Macropus antilopinus*)

All of the macropods are grazing animals. Although they vary in size from around 3 feet / 0.9 meters to as much as 7 feet / 2.13 meters, they all have very large hind legs and powerful, well-muscled tails.

The over-sized hind legs are well designed to allow macropods to cover long distances at a good rate of speed. Hopping, however, is not a matter of strong muscles.

Both kangaroos and wallabies store elastic energy in their tendons, which alternately compress and spring out during hopping. The tendons are responsible for the highly efficient and fast motion, not the muscles.

I'll discuss hopping more fully later in this chapter, but basically a kangaroo's anatomy outfits the animal with a natural internal piston making him a regular engine in motion!

Male kangaroos are called bucks, boomers, or jacks, while the females are does, flyers, or jills. Large groups of kangaroos are called mobs.

Chapter 1 – The World of Marsupials

a.) Red Kangaroo (*Macropus rufus*)

The Red Kangaroo is the largest of its kind and the largest mammal found in Australia. It also has the distinction of being the biggest marsupial in the world.

Red Kangaroos range across most of the Australian mainland, but to a lesser extent in the south, along the east coast, and in the rain forests to the north.

These herbivores (plant eaters) have an average lifespan of 23 years and can weigh as much as 200 lbs. / 90 kg. The length of the head and body is typically 3.25 to 5.25 feet / 1-1.6 meters, although some can reach a maximum height of 7 feet / 2.13 meters.

Even an average-sized Red Kangaroo is as tall as a man and is a seriously impressive animal. They can reach speeds of

35 mph / 56 kph and cover a distance of 25 feet / 8 meters in a single jump.

Red Kangaroos live in the deserts and open grasslands of Australia. Millions are killed annually for meat and for their hides.

b.) Eastern Grey Kangaroo (*Macropus giganteus*)

The Eastern Grey Kangaroo is found in the forests of both Australia and Tasmania. Although they will take to grasslands to graze, they prefer the shelter of trees.

Like the Red Kangaroo, the Eastern Grey is one of the "great kangaroos" due to their impressive size. They, too, can reach a maximum height of 7 feet / 2.13 meters, but are somewhat smaller bodied than their cousins the Reds, weighing around 120 lbs. / 54 kg.

An Eastern Grey's maximum speed is 35 mph / 56 kph, and their life expectancy is 8-10 years. They can cover 25 feet / 8 meters in one leap and can also jump 6 feet / 1.8 meters high.

c.) Western Grey Kangaroo (*Macropus fuliginosus*)

Western Grey Kangaroos are found across all of southern Australia. They are night feeders, preferring grasses, and forage from leafy shrubs and low-hanging tree branches. Nicknamed "stinkers," mature male Western Greys smell distinctly like curry.

Chapter 1 – The World of Marsupials

A sub-species, the Kangaroo Island Kangaroo (*Macropus fuliginosus fuliginosus*) is, appropriately, found only on Kangaroo Island.

Western Greys average 62-119 lbs. / 28-54 kg in weight and have a standing height of as much as 4.3 feet / 1.3 meters. Their lifespan in the wild is as much as 20 years.

You may also see this species referred to as the Black-Faced Kangaroo. In captivity, they will interbreed with the Eastern Grey Kangaroo, but this behavior is never seen in the wild.

d.) Antilopine Kangaroo (*Macropus antilopinus*)

The Antilopine Kangaroo, often called the Antilopine Wallaroo or Antilopine Wallaby is indigenous to northern

Australia and the Kimberley area of Western Australia. "Antilopine" means "antelope like."

Males of the species have a reddish color, with females being grayer in tone. Their coats are shaggy and coarse.

Antilopine Kangaroos resemble both the Red and the Grey Kangaroo, but are taller and slimmer with the bare muzzle more typically seen in wallaroos.

Males will weigh more than 154 lbs. / 70 kg, while the smaller females average around 65 lbs. / 30 kg. Their lifespan in the wild is 10-15 years.

3.) Physical Characteristics of Macropods

Although each of the species of kangaroo differs in subtle ways, there are some general physical characteristics that are the same for all of them. Kangaroos have powerful hind legs and shorter forelegs, but both sets are equipped with sharp claws.

Their senses are extremely keen. If you watch a group of alert kangaroos, you'll see that their ears swivel like a cat's to directionally pick up and interpret sounds.

They are good swimmers, but are completely incapable of moving backwards. This hardly matters, however, since in forward motion, kangaroos are among the most remarkable of all terrestrial creatures.

Chapter 1 – The World of Marsupials

a.) The Mechanics of Hopping

The kangaroo is the only large animal that uses hopping as its primary means of locomotion. Although the physical size difference is considerable, a kangaroo is twice as fast as the other well-known "hopper" of the animal world, the rabbit.

It would be more accurate, however, to describe a kangaroo's motion as similar to that of a child's pogo stick than the kind of forward leaping motion rabbits exhibit.

The fourth toe of a kangaroo's hind foot is elongated and sits in line with the leg bone, which allows the animal to efficiently propel itself off the ground.

The tendons in the legs are highly elastic and are capable of storing energy. When the kangaroo hits the ground, the tendons compress and take in all the available energy of the impact, which is then released on the rebound.

Imagine that the tendon is a spring that gets pushed down as far as it will go and then bursts open as soon as it's released.

The tail's role in all of this is to counterbalance the hind feet. When the kangaroo lands, the tail raises up, then moves to a near vertical position to help out with the upward propulsion.

Researchers have determined that when moving at high rates of speed, kangaroos are the most energy efficient animals on the planet. The faster a roo goes, the farther it hops, so its speed is not a factor of increased muscle motion but rather how much distance a roo can cover in a single leap.

The animals' hearts are huge, more than twice the size of any other creature of comparable body mass, giving kangaroos a lot of physical endurance once they get going.

As it hops, the kangaroo's stomach muscles also expand and contract, forcing air out of the lungs and drawing it back in with no extra energy used.

Chapter 1 – The World of Marsupials

At lower speeds, roos use a motion called a pentapedal walk. A kangaroo never walks on all fours unless it's swimming because the hind legs do not move independently of one another, instead, the tail is used as a balancing fifth leg while the roo shifts forward with the smaller front legs.

This is the motion most commonly seen in grazing groups of kangaroos when they seem to shuffle forward bent over.

b.) Grazing Herbivores

Kangaroos are extremely adaptable to habitat and can go for long periods of time without drinking water, getting the moisture they need from the plants they eat.
A roo's molars or jaw teeth fall out on a regular basis from the wear and tear of its grinding, plant-based diet. The new teeth grow back in, however, unlike other herbivores and grazing ruminants that lose the ability to eat as they grow old because their teeth are so worn down they can't chew any more.

Chapter 2 – Kangaroos in the Wild

In Australia, all the states and territories have laws in place to protect kangaroos. Licensed hunters harvest the four major species of kangaroo for export according to an approved government plan of management.

There is no kangaroo farming industry. Only wild specimens are taken for various uses including for their meat and hides.

Although it is legal to offer assistance to an orphaned joey, you will require a permit to keep the animal and raise it in captivity.

Because kangaroos, especially Eastern Greys, adapt very well to changed landscapes, they are routinely encountered

Chapter 2 – Kangaroos in the Wild

on heavily trafficked areas like golf courses, cemeteries, parks, farmland, and residential areas.

All a roo really wants to be happy is shelter, water and grass. These social animals congregate in groups called mobs and, while tolerant of a human presence, can become aggressive under certain circumstances.

1.) Potential Aggression

Paradoxically, some of the most problematic roos are the very ones that are most used to interaction with human beings. A kangaroo that is used to accepting food from humans can get downright aggressive if you don't have something for him!

Humans are discouraged from interacting with kangaroos except under approved conditions. It's also important to recognize situations in which an encounter with a roo can get out of hand so you can avoid trouble at all costs.

Adult males that are fighting to gain higher status in a mob are also prone to showing aggression. The dominant male in a mob will father all of the joeys in the next generation of breeding, so this is a rather important "contest" in the kangaroo world

Getting too close to a dominant male can lead to a confrontational reaction, especially with Eastern Greys since they mate year round.

Chapter 2 – Kangaroos in the Wild

Females that still have a joey in the pouch can also become defensive if they feel their offspring is being threatened in some way.

2.) Handling Aggressive Behavior

If a kangaroo behaves toward you in an aggressive way, do not turn your back on the animal and do not run.

A kangaroo can easily and effortlessly outdistance a running human, and they can kick you while they're in motion.

Avoid eye contact with the animal, which the roo may take as a challenge. Slowly back away. Crouch or keep your head down.

Chapter 2 – Kangaroos in the Wild

It is also useful to emit a short, deep cough, which is, in the roo's "language" an acknowledgement of his dominance over you.

3.) Watch, Don't Interact

The overall placid appearance of a kangaroo in the wild can be deeply misleading. They seem gentle to the point of boredom, staring back at you while thoughtfully chewing their cud.

Don't be fooled by appearances. Roos can and do react with lightning speed. Even a gentle wild roo that has become accustomed to accepting food from humans can be dangerous.

They just don't realize how big they are, or that we humans aren't sturdy enough to be dealt with in proper roo fashion!

The best course of action with roos in the "wild," even if that is your own backyard or the neighborhood park is to watch, but not interact. Avoid the temptation to feed wild roos, and do nothing to incite aggression.

The bitter truth is that in any interaction with a human, the wild animal will take the blame and pay the consequences no matter what inappropriate thing the person did to provoke or interest the animal.

For your own safety and for that of the roos, that far prefer to just go about minding their own business and being

Chapter 2 – Kangaroos in the Wild

kangaroos, keep your relationship with macropods in the wild at a safe and appreciative distance.

Chapter 3 – What to Know Before Buying

Obviously the decision to keep a kangaroo as a pet is far different than choosing to adopt a dog or a cat. There are numerous things to consider well in advance of buying a roo.

1.) Do I Need a License?

Kangaroos are considered exotic animals and are therefore subject to the laws in your country regarding the keeping of non-native species.

One of the first steps you must take in contemplating roo ownership is an investigation of the applicable legal ramifications.

Chapter 3 – What to Know Before Buying

Failure to read up on and to understand the laws in question will undoubtedly result in a heavy fine for you and seizure and perhaps death for an innocent animal.

a.) Laws in the U.S.

The term "exotic" in the United States is subject to constantly shifting legal definition. In the most basic sense, an exotic is a non-native species. The operative definitions vary from one jurisdiction to the next, however.

Federal law stipulates than an exotic species is "an animal that is native to a foreign country or of foreign origin or character, is not native to the United States, or was introduced from abroad."

The need to obtain a license or a permit will vary considerably from one state to the next. Some states impose an outright ban on the possession of any exotic animal while others draw often arbitrary and conflicting lines of demarcation.

Overview of State Exotic Animal Laws:

As of late 2013, the following broad categories for exotic animal legislation per state were accurate. Bear in mind, however, that statutes are subject to change at any time. Find out the exact law in your state BEFORE purchasing a kangaroo.

Chapter 3 – What to Know Before Buying

States That Ban Most Captive Exotics

California
Colorado
Georgia
Illinois
Iowa
Kentucky
New Mexico
New Hampshire
New York
New Jersey
Maryland
Oregon
Washington
Utah

States That Allow Designated Species

Arkansas
Kansas
Florida
Maine
Louisiana
Michigan
Minnesota
Montana
Nebraska
Wyoming
Tennessee

States That Require Permits

Arizona
Idaho
North Dakota
South Dakota
Oklahoma
Texas
Missouri
Mississippi
Indiana
Pennsylvania
Virginia
Rhode Island

States with No Restrictions

Nevada
Wisconsin
Ohio
West Virginia
North Carolina
South Carolina

b.) Licensing in the U.K.

In reaction to the increased popularity of exotic species, the United Kingdom passed the Dangerous Wild Animals Act in 1976. The law regulates the keeping of primates, carnivores, large reptiles, spiders, scorpions, and several species of marsupials including kangaroos.

Chapter 3 – What to Know Before Buying

To keep these animals legally, a license must be purchased for a fee. Other stipulations will vary by region. Contact your local council to obtain a precise understanding of the relevant regulations.

For the full text of the Dangerous Wild Animals Act 1976, please see: www.legislation.gov.uk/ukpga/1976/38

2.) Keeping Multiple Kangaroos?

Obviously the dominant limiting factor in considering the keeping of multiple kangaroos is space. I cannot emphasize strongly enough that kangaroos, no matter how docile, are wild animals that need a considerable amount of room outdoors to feed, live, and exercise.

It is true that kangaroos are social creatures that enjoy being with their own kind. If you do decide to keep multiples, it's better to keep females than multiple males to lessen the chances of aggressive behavior.

If you do plan to keep multiple kangaroos, make sure the enclosure you provide, and the pasture to which they have access is large enough for their needs. Observe the animals closely in the beginning to make sure everyone is getting along.

3.) Kangaroos and Other Pets?

For the most part kangaroos, once fully grown, will do quite well with non-aggressive dogs although a young joey can be seriously injured by a family pet that is simply playing too hard.

Don't leave the animals unsupervised, even when you think they're all on amiable terms. Animals react in the moment, and tend to respond to aggression with aggression, especially if they are injured or in pain.

Chapter 3 – What to Know Before Buying

Kangaroos should NOT be kept with cats. Feline feces can contain the protozoan that causes toxoplasmosis even if the cat appears to be completely healthy. This condition is fatal to kangaroos, with young joeys being especially vulnerable.

4.) Cost of Care

The greatest initial expense in acquiring a kangaroo will be the price of the animal itself. During the first year of life, your roo can probably live indoors, but then you will be faced with constructing an appropriate outdoor enclosure.

a.) Initial Costs

The following are the projected initial costs for becoming a kangaroo owner.

Purchase Price

The cost of buying a kangaroo from a breeder will vary greatly depending on location and availability. The animals are fairly scarce outside their native Australia.

Expect to pay, on average, $1000-$4000+ (£646 to £2585+).

Vaccinations

It is generally not necessary to have a kangaroo vaccinated. If the procedure is required, costs will range from $50-$100 (£37 to £75) per injection.

Food/Water Containers

In your kangaroo's enclosure you will need a free standing or wall mounted hay rack, a trough, and water containers. Plastic or aluminum work well for all these receptacles. Each one will cost from $100 to $150 (£65 - £97).

Pen/Shed

Depending on size, materials used, bedding, shelter and furnishings, expect to spend $500-$2000 (£323 - £1293) on your kangaroo's pen and shed.

Multiple kangaroos will sleep in one big pile so if you have more than one roo, make sure the shelter is large enough for a big slumber party!

b.) Monthly Expenses

The following items are the major monthly costs you will encounter in keeping a kangaroo:

Food

Food for one kangaroo will cost $100 to $200 (£65 - £129) per month. The prices for individual foods break down as:

horse or "pony" cubes
$45-$50 / £25-£31 for 88 lbs. / 40 kgs

alfalfa hay*
$225 / £8 per ton (2000 lbs./907 kg)

Obviously you will be buying hay in bales, broken down from a per ton price or priced per bale.

kangaroo muesli or mixed food
wallabies and wallaroos
$45 / £28 per 77 lbs. / 35 kgs.

Veterinary Services

Often when seeking veterinary aid for a kangaroo it is necessary for the vet to come to you. Prices will vary depending on the illness or injury, but the cost for the visit itself averages $50 (£37.40) or more.

Chapter 3 – What to Know Before Buying

Purchasing a kangaroo is not as easy as going to your local pet store. You may not be able to find a breeder in your area.

If this is the case, I strongly advise against having a joey shipped to you. It would be far preferable for you to drive to the breeding establishment to pick up the animal.

Young joeys are shy and sensitive by nature. They are extremely susceptible to changes in temperature and humidity, and crave the feeling of security that comes with growing up in their mother's pouch.

Chapter 3 – What to Know Before Buying

For these and other reasons, many breeders will not even consider shipping the animals, so you may need to factor travel costs into your initial purchase expense.

5.) Buying in the U.S.

In the United States, you will need to find a breeder in order to get a legal animal in good health. The following breeders offer various kangaroo species.

While this list is not comprehensive, you may be able to contact these breeders to make contact with a facility closer to your location.

Deer Park Exotics
Contact: Perry Viator
Email: boomeroo@att.net
Phone: 409-656-9705
Website: www.deerparkexotics.com
Red Kangaroos

Buffalo Hill Exotics
Contact: Larry & Judy Rohner
Email: buffalohillexotics@netwitz.net
Phone: 618-532-9036
Website: www.buffalohillexotics
Dama Wallabies, Bennett's Wallabies, Red Kangaroos

Tri Lakes Exotics
Contact: Cathy Cranmore
Email: cathy@trilakesexotics.com
Phone: 903-588-2727

Website: www.trilakesexotics.com
Red Kangaroo and Wallaroos.

Castleberry Safari Ltd
Contact: Janice Castleberry
Email: janice@castleberrysafariltd.com
Phone: 512-639-4087
Website: www.castleberrysafariltd.com
Red Kangaroos

Sandstone Mountain Ranch
Contact: Ranch Office
Email: SandstoneRanch@aol.com
Phone: 325-247-4252
Website: sandstonemountainranch.homestead.com
Red Kangaroos

6.) Buying in the U.K.

Because the keeping of kangaroos is so heavily regulated in the United Kingdom, contacting dealers is somewhat more difficult.

Chapter 3 – What to Know Before Buying

7.) Buying a Healthy Kangaroo

Some of the things to look for in a healthy kangaroo you are considering for purchase include:

- Bright and alert eyes
- No signs of illness or injury
- Smooth motion without limping or dragging
- Even temperament
- Displays no fear of humans
- No discharge from the eyes, nose or mouth
- Healthy appetite
- No signs of diarrhea in the enclosure
- Coat is in good condition

Pros and Cons of Owning a Kangaroo

Any time you consider an exotic animal as a pet it's important to understand that what is a "pro" for one person may be a "con" for another, which means the following list is somewhat subjective.

Pros of Kangaroos

- If well socialized, roos can be friendly and social
- Will often respond to simple commands
- Easy to feed with readily available commercial diets
- Affectionate with their humans
- Unique and entertaining pets
- Joeys can be hand-raised on formula
- Tend to be gentle by nature

Cons of Kangaroos

- Can grow quite large
- Require adequate outdoor space
- Mischievous if not properly supervised
- Expensive to purchase
- Subject to legal restrictions in given areas

Chapter 4 – Keeping Kangaroos as Pets

If you decide to keep a kangaroo as a pet, the two major things you have to worry about are where your roo will live and what he will eat. If you can manage those two things well, kangaroos will thrive in captivity and become very tame and affectionate with their human friends.

1.) A Joey's First Year

If you get your kangaroo from a breeder, you'll be sent home with everything you need to raise your new pet including a pouch, the right kind of bottle outfitted with a marsupial nipple, and a recommended milk supplement.

Most breeders also have instruction sheets and other written materials to help you act as a stand-in parent for

Chapter 4 – Keeping Kangaroos as Pets

your new joey, and they're happy to answer questions because they want to see your little pet do well.

a.) Milk Replacers

If you're rescuing an orphaned joey, you'll have to pick up all those supplies on your own. Since joeys cannot tolerate cow's milk, it's important that you immediately get the right milk replacement product. The best source is:

Wombaroo.com / Perfect Pets Inc.
www.perfectpet.net/wombaroo/index.html (US)
www.wombaroo.com.au (Australia)

Please note that this company will also ship internationally. If you're in Australia, many veterinary offices carry milk replacement products, and you can also find them in feed stores.

The companies that make these products create growth charts to help you decide which grade of the supplement to use and how much to feed.

Mother kangaroos have the ability to change how their milk is produced so that the joey gets the right level of nutrition as it grows. The milk replacement products try to recreate that process, so you must follow the feeding guidelines on the product precisely.

When you're taking care of a joey, you might as well have a newborn baby in the house. The little fellow needs to spend as much time with you in its pouch as possible to get the same kind of bonding and security it would get from being with its mother.

b.) A Substitute Pouch

Joeys are happiest when you just put on the pouch and wear it. This lets the baby benefit from the warmth of your body, and to think of you as "Mum." Bottle fed joeys are extremely loyal and affectionate because you rapidly become their "family."

Most people who have no experience with kangaroos are shocked at what good pets they will make, and how much they love their humans.

If you are helping an orphan joey, you can use a soft, clean blanket as a temporary pouch, but you will want to quickly find a commercial product.

Chapter 4 – Keeping Kangaroos as Pets

These surrogate pouches are well designed, easily washed, and come in varying sizes to grow with your joey. Pouches sell for $20-$50 / £12-£30.

Make sure that the pouch you are using is big enough for the joey to move around, but also to feel snug. The pouch should always be suspended.

Never let the bottom touch the floor, but when you're not with the baby, the pouch should be low enough for the little guy to safely jump in and out on his own.

c.) Maintaining the Correct Temperature

Little joeys can't control their own body temperature. The baby will rely on you to provide consistent warmth until it has a good layer of fur in place. Inside the mother's pouch the joey would enjoy a toasty 86-90 F / 30-32 C.

A small heating pad placed outside the pouch and regulated with intervening layers of material will let you accurately adjust the temperature for your joey.

As an example, Wombaroo sells a "Cosy Heat Pad" measuring 102" x 14.2" / 260mm x 360mm. The unit is specifically designed for use with baby marsupials, and retails for approximately $89 / £55.

The pad heats to 59-68 F / 15-20 C above the ambient temperature of the room. Be sure to monitor the temperature inside the pouch, however, not in the room.

Do not allow the joey to get overheated. Heat stress can be fatal.

d.) Feeding Your Joey

If you buy your joey from a breeder, you'll come home with the right feeding equipment. If you're on your own, however, you'll need to get a proper bottle and marsupial nipple.

Joeys have tender mouths and gums. A hard rubber teat will injure their mouths and cause sores to erupt. Marsupial nipples are available from companies and stores selling milk replacement products and cost less than $2 / £1.22 each.

Feed the joey in the pouch sitting on your lap. If the baby is not already accustomed to eating from a bottle cup your hand gently under its chin and cover its eyes with your hand.

This will help the baby to settle down to eat. It may also be necessary to open the joey's mouth with your thumb to insert the nipple.

Never squeeze the bottle thinking this will entice the baby to eat. You run the risk of getting liquid in the joey's lungs, which is extremely dangerous.

Feed according to the schedule recommended for the supplemental milk product you are using.

Chapter 4 – Keeping Kangaroos as Pets

e.) Toileting

When the joey has finished feeding, remove the baby from the pouch and carry it to the toilet. In the wild, the mother kangaroo would lick the joey's anal area to stimulate urination and defecation.

Tap or gently stroke the area with a damp washcloth or tissue to replicate this action. It is extremely important that joeys be toiled regularly, especially after feedings and upon waking.

If a joey is not toileted with sufficient frequency, they can be subject to urinary tract and bowel disorders.

f.) Weaning

Most experts are in agreement that joeys should be allowed to continue feeding from a bottle as long as they like. In time, they will tire of a liquid diet and begin to exhibit an interest in solid foods naturally.

You can begin to offer the joey tiny pieces of green grass to kindle its interest in an adult diet.

(Please see Chapter 6 on Hand Rearing a Joey for more information on transitional feeding.)

g.) Playpens

It's a good idea during your joey's first year to use a child's playpen to help contain your pet. Soon enough the joey will need to be moved to an outside enclosure. While it's inside, however, a playpen will give your pet a safe place to be outside your supervision.

Suspend the joey's pouch securely from one corner, making sure it's low enough to the base of the pen that the joey can safely jump in and out.

This arrangement not only protects the joey from other pets and from household hazards, but from himself. Joeys are insatiably curious and prone to getting themselves into trouble!

2.) Becoming an Adult

As the joey matures, it will naturally begin to develop an interest in solid foods. Encourage nibbling behavior on soft

Chapter 4 – Keeping Kangaroos as Pets

plant material in limited quantities as a transition to the adult foods that will be your pet's staples for life.

Your pet kangaroo will eat a diet comprised of equal parts hay, kangaroo muesli, and cubes or "cake."

a.) Types of Food

In addition to the staples, your kangaroo may also be interested in:

- rolled oats
- grass (with the roots attached)
- dairy meal
- carrots and celery
- sweet potatoes
- apples

When feeding grains, make sure they are crushed. Also, do not feed your kangaroo large amounts of fresh grass. Use clean, dry hay only.

Additionally, commercial pellets (also called cubes or "cake") will be an important part of your pet's diet. The typical nutritional breakdown of these items is:

- Crude protein, min. 14.0%
- Crude fat, min. 3.0%
- Crude fiber, max. 13.0%
- Actual salt 0.75%
- Fluorine, max. 0.0096%

Choose a hay like Lucerne / alfalfa that is high in dietary fiber. Beware of low quality hays that are filled with chaff and sharp pieces that can harm the kangaroo's tender mouth.

b.) Dispensing Food

Sturdy, solid containers that will prevent food from being scattered or spoiled and that are easily cleaned are your best choice. Either plastic or aluminum pans will work well for both food and water.

Make sure that the water containers are large enough to allow the kangaroo to completely immerse his forelegs, something they like to do on hot days to help them cool down.

Use a bin or a trough for pellet foods, and a free-standing or wall-mounted hayrack.

3.) Outside Enclosure Requirements

Sometime during or shortly after the first year of life, your kangaroo will be too big to keep in the house. You will need to design an outside enclosure that will keep your pet safe from predators, prevent it from escaping, and be both a comfortable and natural home.

With any enclosure for a captive animal, bigger is better. Kangaroos can do well in a large pen, but a fenced pasture is ideal.

The recommended minimum area for two kangaroos is 820 feet^2 (250 m^2). For each additional animal introduced, this space should be increased by 18 feet^2 (5.50 m^2).

a.) Fencing

In areas with a strong population of predators, consider double fencing. An outer electric fence can keep predators from getting close enough to dig under the primary fence and attack your kangaroo.

Although kangaroos are known for their ability to jump, it's crucial to understand that they have a tendency to try to go through fences, not over them.

Don't create any kind of barrier around your roo's enclosure that can pose a threat to your pet's safety.

Chapter 4 – Keeping Kangaroos as Pets

Your fence should be:

- 6.5 feet (2 m) tall
- constructed with a buried 1.5 ft. (0.5 m) lower section
- include a 1.5 ft (0.5 m) outer overhang at a 45-degree angle

Make sure there are no gaps that will attract the roo's curious eye and no spaces in which they can get their heads or forelimbs caught.

Planting bushes in the corners can protect roos from becoming agitated and crashing into the support posts.

b.) Holding Area

Incorporating a small holding area or yard is a good idea. This space, secured by a gate, will be handy when you need to confine your kangaroo.

Chapter 4 – Keeping Kangaroos as Pets

This necessity might arise for medical reasons or to keep the animal safe while work is being done on the enclosure. Any situation that raises the potential for stress and/or escape, a holding area can make all the difference.

Consider including some option for visual barriers in the holding area like shade cloths that will make your pet feel more secure by limiting its view of activities in the surrounding area.

c.) Shelters

Depending on the climate, your roo will be happy with either a lean-to shelter or an actual barn (with heat as needed). Make sure that the roo can get under cover and be protected from inclement weather approaching from any direction.

For any enclosure or lean-to, make sure the area is large enough for all kangaroos present. They will sleep in one big pile no matter what you do, so give them enough room!

d.) Furnishings

The shelter in the enclosure should have a soft substrate that will compact easily. Don't use bare concrete. The best option is a grassy yard planted with a mix of summer and winter grasses.

Use logs and leafy branches for decorations as well as hard plastic cylinders, balls, and other means of recreation and intellectual stimulation.

Kangaroos actually like their creature comforts and will be quite happy if you scatter a number of large, soft dog beds throughout their enclosure.

Just experiment with "toys." Roos are very curious and will display an immediate interest in something that captures their imagination. As long as the item poses no danger to them, almost anything will work as a kangaroo "toy" as long as the roo himself approves!

4.) Suggested Maintenance

The cleaner you keep your kangaroo's habitat, the happier and healthier your pet will be. Always wash your hands BEFORE handling or feeding your pets. Clean the feeding area each day, and remove all debris from the enclosure.

Use the following suggested schedules as guidelines only. Clean often and clean well!

Daily:

- Fill all water containers with clean, fresh water
- Clean the food troughs/pans
- Rake and remove accumulated feces
- Remove all other debris

Chapter 4 – Keeping Kangaroos as Pets

2-3 Times a Week:

- Scrub water containers
- Disinfect food troughs/pans
- Replace provided bedding like hay
- Clean shed/barn walls

Keep a regular schedule of these maintenance tasks on a calendar to be sure that each is performed according to plan. The stricter you are with your upkeep schedule the healthier your kangaroos will be.

Chapter 5 – Kangaroo Reproduction

When scientists first began to try to understand how kangaroos reproduce and raise their young, many of their theories pointed to a birth inside the pouch. The initial belief was that the young joey came into the world attached to its mother's teat.

It is true that the nipple swells inside the young kangaroo's mouth. If the joey is removed too soon, or with any force, the baby can be seriously injured to the point of bleeding to death.

But there is no truth to the idea that the joey actually forms in the pouch. The reality of the process is much more miraculous. When a joey emerges from the womb, it is a tiny neonate, no larger than a bean.

Chapter 5 – Kangaroo Reproduction

The baby begins life by arduously crawling up its mother's body and into the womb where it finds the teat on its own, latches on, and begins the next stages of its physical development.

1.) Kangaroo Breeding

Breeding kangaroos in captivity is, to some extent, simply a matter of allowing nature to take its course. Most people who keep a pet kangaroo will not be breeding the animal, but understanding this aspect of macropod biology offers fascinating insight into just how unique these creatures are in the animal kingdom.

a.) Fertility

Female kangaroos have a remarkable ability to control their reproductive cycles via a process called embryonic diapause. Females are fertile year round at 35 day intervals. Neither an existing pregnancy nor having a joey in the pouch interrupts fertility.

If a female kangaroo has one joey in the pouch, she can become pregnant again, but the embryo stops developing and exists in a state of limbo waiting. When the older offspring leaves the womb, development resumes, and as soon as that baby is born, the female is ready to conceive again.

This process of "embryonic diapause" can also be activated by adverse environmental conditions, and is thus an aspect of the kangaroo's ability to survive in the harsh and arid climate of its native Australia.

Chapter 5 – Kangaroo Reproduction

Even with this kind of protective adaptation, about 50% of joeys born in the wild do not survive to two years of age. Many fall prey to goannas (large lizards), dingoes, pythons, and wedge-tailed eagles.

2.) Mating and Birth

Kangaroos do not mate for life. A male will have several female partners. In fact, the dominant male in a mob fathers the entire generation of joeys for that group so long as he remains dominant.

A female kangaroo does not exhibit any external signs of pregnancy. In the hours before giving birth, she will clean her pouch by leaning forward and sticking her head inside.

In the birth position, her tail will pass between her hind legs, and her hind quarters will rest on the ground. The female leans into a vertical object, like a tree trunk, to support her back.

Birth occurs about 33 days after mating. The neonate's head appears still enclosed in the amniotic sac, which is either broken open by the action of the mother's licking, or by the young using a claw to rupture the tissue.

The tiny, hairless neonate emerges from the amniotic sac and begins to climb up a trail the mother has licked into her fur for the joey to follow.

Chapter 5 – Kangaroo Reproduction

(Please note that there is debate about whether or not the mother kangaroo's licking actually helps to direct her baby's journey to the pouch. Some sources say that as she cleans, she sometimes licks over the neonate, which makes it look as if she's helping out, when in reality this is not the case.)

3.) Journey to the Pouch

The little joey makes its way up the mother's body by grasping her fur in its tiny forelegs. The back legs are not yet developed and provide no assistance to the neonate. The baby's body moves from side to side as it crawls upward.

For at least a portion of the journey, the umbilical cord is still attached to the neonate. The tension of being stretched

Chapter 5 – Kangaroo Reproduction

in addition to licking by the mother will finally sever the cord.

When the baby reaches the pouch, it disappears inside and locates one of the mother's four teats, where it immediately attaches itself. Remarkably, the entire journey takes less than 3 minutes, although it can be as long as 15 minutes before the neonate finds the nipple.

During this process, the mother seems to be oblivious to the presence of her tiny baby. She is occupied with licking away all the birth fluids and blood, efficiently removing any evidence of the process from her fur.

4.) In the Pouch

At the point at which the joey enters the pouch, it has well-developed front legs, a strong jaw, and a well-muscled tongue.

Neither the eyes nor the ears are functional, but the nostrils are large because the sense of smell is apparently essential for the joey to find its way up the mother's body.

The joey will spend the next 190 days drawing nourishment from the mother, and will remain in the pouch to some extent for a total of 235 days on average.

The mother will keep the pouch clean as the joey continues to develop by inserting her muzzle and licking the area many times a day. The bigger the baby becomes, the stronger the maternal-infant bond grows.

Chapter 5 – Kangaroo Reproduction

When the joey begins to start exploring the world, the mother will help her young get back in the pouch by bending down and spreading her forelegs. If necessary, she will hunch down closer to the ground.

Joeys dive head first into the pouch, then turn a perfect somersault, and pop their heads back out immediately to have a look around.

If during these "outside" excursions the joey gets lost, the mother will call loudly, or the baby will cry for Mama to come to the rescue — a sound to which all of the female kangaroos in the area will respond.

5.) Pouch Life Ends

When the joey's pouch life comes to an end, the mother kangaroo often has to restrain the baby by grasping it

Chapter 5 – Kangaroo Reproduction

firmly with her front legs. She's not only encouraging independence, but protecting her next offspring.

If a large joey were to jump in the pouch after the next neonate is in place, the force of the entry could kill the fragile baby.

If a mother can't get her big joey out of the pouch any other way, she simply relaxes her muscles and dumps the little fellow out on the ground.

At this stage of its growth, the joey should be a robust 8.5-11 lbs. / 4-5 kg. The mother will allow her young to suckle from outside the pouch for another four months, until it's about a year old.

During this time, the joey follows close on its mother's heels, and it will continue to stay in close association with her even after being weaned.

Chapter 6 – Hand Rearing a Joey

Although the process differs slightly with rescued joeys versus pets purchased from a breeder, all baby kangaroos take a lot of care from their surrogate "mothers."

1.) Rescued Joeys

If you are helping a joey that has been orphaned due to an accident of some sort, be sure to keep the animal warm and get it to a qualified veterinarian as soon as possible.

The joey will also be suffering from stress due to separation from its mother and lack of nourishment. It's important to get the baby into a substitute pouch at the correct temperature.

Chapter 6 – Hand Rearing a Joey

a.) A Word on Handling

It's a normal human reaction to want to comfort a small creature by cuddling it. You must resist this temptation with an orphaned kangaroo. Minimize handling the joey until it's safely in a substitute pouch. The feeling of safety will help lower the animal's stress level.

An orphaned joey needs peace and quiet. This is especially critical if you have children in the house, and an excellent opportunity to teach them the value of kindness and patience in caring for animals.

The joey must be allowed to recover from the stress of separation and to develop a level of comfort in its new surroundings. This will greatly enhance the baby's chances of surviving and remaining healthy.

2.) A Substitute Pouch

When hand raised joeys need a substitute pouch made of soft, easily washable material. This can be anything from an old blanket to commercially designed pouches retailing for $20-$50 US / £12-£30.

The pouch should be large enough for the joey to move around, but also for the little animal to stay snug. The pouch should be suspended.

Don't let the bottom touch the ground, but keep the whole unit close enough to the floor so that when the joey is old enough to jump out, it can do so on its own.

Chapter 6 – Hand Rearing a Joey

3.) Regulating Temperature

It's crucial to understand that a joey has no way to regulate its own body temperature. The baby will rely on you to provide it with an external heat source.

When joeys stay with their mothers, they don't leave the pouch until they have a good layer of fur on their bodies. The temperature inside the mother's pouch is a toasty 86-90 F / 30-32 C.

The best way to ensure that a joey stays warm in a substitute pouch is to use a small electric blanket outside the pouch itself.

Wombaroo offers a "Cosy Heat Pad" that measures 102" x 14.2" / 260mm x 360mm. It is designed specifically for use with orphaned marsupials. The temperature at the surface of the pad reaches 59-68 F / 15-20 C above the ambient room temperature.

Chapter 6 – Hand Rearing a Joey

You can adjust the amount of heat the joey receives from a pad of this kind by increasing or decreasing layers of material between the pad and the rearing pouch.

Always monitor the inside of the pouch with a thermometer. Allowing the temperature to climb too high will cause the joey to suffer from heat stress.

4.) Diet and Nutrition

A mother kangaroo's milk is highly specialized, changing over the course of her baby's development to provide the correct level of nourishment.

Milk replacement products for joeys are rated according to age in an effort to match this natural means of supporting the animal's growth.

Using Wombaroo Food Products again as an example, the company has developed a series of growth charts recommending grade of food to be used and amounts to be dispensed.

The food itself is packaged as a dry powder that will last 24 months in storage. For use, water is added.
Joeys should always be fed in their pouches and then removed and taken to the toilet. As orphan joeys are getting used to taking a bottle, they may struggle.

Gently cup your hand under the baby's chin and cover its eyes. This will quiet the joey and get it to settle down to nurse.

Chapter 6 – Hand Rearing a Joey

5.) Selecting a Teat

Joeys have very tender mouths and are subject to the formation of ulcers and other small irritations. You can't use normal baby teats or any kind of hard rubber to feed a joey.

It's important to secure teats from a company like Wombaroo that are specifically designed for use with kangaroos. If you are in an emergency situation, use an eye dropper to hand feed the joy, or find the softest bit of rubber tubing available.

It's imperative that the correct teat be located as soon as possible.

Chapter 7 – Kangaroo Health

Learning to recognize the symptoms of disease and injury is an important aspect of preventive medicine that will help you to keep your kangaroo healthy. In all cases, the more rapidly treatment is administered, the greater the chances of recovery.

1.) Common Health Problems

If well fed and kept in clean conditions, kangaroos tend to be healthy animals, although they are somewhat sensitive to stress. When health problems do arise, the following are the most common issues.

a.) Hair Loss

Kangaroos can experience hair loss from inadequacies in their diet and from stress. In young joeys, an overly warm environment may be the culprit.

Skin irritations and fungal infections are also a potential cause. Be especially careful about bleach in the soap powders used to launder items with which the roo comes into contact.

Treatment for hair loss can be a process of elimination until the correct cause is identified. Wash items with plain soaps, reduce stress levels, and if necessary get a topical anti-fungal cream from the veterinarian.

b.) Flea Infestations

Kangaroos typically only become infested with fleas when they have come into contact with other domestic animals troubled by the parasites. (The same is true of lice.)

The treatment for both of these parasites is carboryl or a pyrethrum-based powder. Other animals with whom the roo comes into contact should also be treated to avoid the chance of a re-infestation.

It should be noted that pyrethrum powders have caused adverse reactions in small dog and cat breeds. For this reason, if a joey is infested with fleas, these products should only be used with the advice of a veterinarian.

c.) Ticks

Ticks are much more dangerous to kangaroos than fleas or lice. If too many ticks accumulate on a kangaroo, the blood loss can cause anemia.

When ticks first attach themselves to a kangaroo, they look like tiny brown seeds. As they become engorged, however, they swell to many times their original size and take on a pale, off-white coloration.

Great care should be taken when removing a tick so that the head is not left behind embedded in the roo's skin where it will cause a festering sore.

First, coat the tick in a thick layer of petroleum jelly to suffocate it and cause the jaws to release. After a few minutes, grasp the tick firmly with a pair of tweezers pulling straight back.

Do not use a twisting motion or the tick's head will disengage and remain behind.

d.) Prolapsed Bowel

Kangaroos suffering from severe diarrhea may also experience a prolapsed bowel. The organ literally extrudes from the body and must be pushed back in place.

Often a bowel prolapse will correct itself within an hour or so, but in some severe instances it will be necessary for a veterinarian to reposition the organ and to secure it in place with a stitch.

e.) Scours or Diarrhea

Diarrhea or "scours" in captive kangaroos typically results from poor hygiene in the enclosure and a low-quality diet. It is also possible for a bacterial or viral infection in the intestines to cause the condition.

In joeys, a case of the scours may be caused by overfeeding or using the wrong food, which the growing animal cannot yet properly digest.

Treatment should be determined by a veterinarian, and will typically include the use of medication, electrolytes, and/or probiotics.

f.) Thrush

Thrush is caused by *Candida Albicans*, and is a yeast infection confirmed by a veterinarian-administered gram stain test.

Initial symptoms include diarrhea, a foul odor, and stools that are yellow/green and/or frothy. As the infection progresses, mouth sores and lesions will become evident as well.

Thrush is caused by poor hygiene, stress, cloaca sucking, or a reaction to antibiotics. The standard treatment is Nilstat at a dose of 0.1 ml per 1 kg / 2.2 lbs. body weight.

(Be aware, however, that Nilstat itself can cause diarrhea for the first three to five days.)

g.) Pneumonia

The two main causes of pneumonia in kangaroos are becoming overly cold or inhaling fluid into the lungs. Joeys are especially susceptible to both.

Symptoms include congestion in the chest, sniffling after feeding, overall listlessness, and a refusal to eat. Treatment in most cases involves the administration of antibiotics, typically Baytril at a dose of 1 mg per 10 kg / 22 lbs. body weight.

Never ignore symptoms of respiratory distress in a kangaroo. Pneumonia can be life threatening for all macropods.

h.) Necrobacillosis (Lumpy Jaw)

Necrobacillosis or "Lumpy Jaw" presents with inflammation of the bone or soft tissues that quickly leads to necrotizing decay. It is caused by *Fusobacterium necrophorum* and is often complicated by secondary concurrent infections.

The bacteria enters the body through a break in the skin. Unfortunately, by the time symptoms become evident, the infected kangaroo is usually near death. Signs will include lesions and ulcerations that leak yellow-green pus and emit a foul odor.

Chapter 7 – Kangaroo Health

It is imperative that veterinary care be administered as quickly as possible. In some instances, the vaccine used to treat foot rot in sheep has proven to be effective, but the prognosis for Lumpy Jaw is not good and euthanasia may be required.

2.) Dealing with Injuries

Kangaroos are lively and curious animals and may well injure themselves. It is important to monitor your pet and address all wounds immediately. Be alert for any of the following warning signs:

- Altered posture or carriage of the body
- Nervous or fearful behavior
- Listless or lethargic behavior
- Limbs held loosely
- Hanging or drooping of the head or ears
- Lack of coordination
- Shaking or convulsions
- Poor condition of the fur
- Coughing, sneezing, vomiting
- Any signs of blood on the animal or in the pen
- Change in color or consistency of feces

If any of these signs are present, carefully examine the kangaroo to locate potential injury. Take the following precautions to minimize stress:

- Conduct all examinations in a safe area
- Keep the animal as quiet as possible
- Have what you need laid out and ready, don't leave the kangaroo alone
- Work quickly and systematically from one side of the body to the other
- Compare both sides to identify differences that could signal injury
- Stop immediately if the kangaroo becomes agitated or seems to be going into shock

Common signs of stress include:

- Marked changes up or down in level of activity
- Attempts to escape
- Thumping with the feet or tail against the ground

Chapter 7 – Kangaroo Health

- Barking, hissing, or grinding the teeth
- Shaking the head or flicking the ears
- Changes in body temperature
- Licking the chest, forearms, or shoulders
- Clawing at the body
- Diarrhea, especially in young joeys
- Decreased appetite

3.) Administering First Aid

The basic principles of first aid for kangaroos or really any companion animal are prioritized in the same fashion as a response to human medical emergencies.

1. Safety of the patient
2. Safety of the bystanders
3. Prevention of further injury

Although other people who are present may have good intentions in offering their assistance, note that an injured and frightened animal can react with even greater fear to an unknown presence. Unless you need additional physical aid, it's best to work with your pet alone.

Taking the following steps in this order:

1. Clear the airway (if blocked)
2. Stop the bleeding
3. Maintain body temperature
4. Minimize stress

Attempt to treat any wounds or fractures only after these steps have been accomplished.

a.) Clear the Airway

If you can do so safely, gently remove obstructions from the mouth. If you cannot accomplish this task, you must get the animal to a veterinarian.

If no obstruction is present, put the kangaroo in a safe area, keep your pet warm, and observe his behavior. If the kangaroo is unconscious, lay him on his side with his head lowered, but still at a level higher than the stomach.

This angle keeps the larynx open and allows fluids to drain. Check that the animal's nostrils are open and if necessary, clear away any debris.

b.) Stop the Bleeding

Apply firm pressure to an open wound with your hands or a bandage. If the kangaroo is struggling, try to calm your pet. Physical activity will cause the heart to pump even more blood.
If you can't staunch the flow with pressure, cover the wound with a soft dressing and secure it in place with a bandage. Get your pet to a veterinarian as soon as possible.

Be careful not to let any bandage obstruct the kangaroo's ability to breathe.

Chapter 7 – Kangaroo Health

c.) Maintain Body Temperature

Under normal circumstances, marsupials have a lower body temperature than humans, around 95-97°F (35-36°C). Their temperature will drop even more if they are injured and going into shock.

Maintaining their body temperature to prevent this from happening is crucial, however you MUST NOT allow a macropod to become overheated. Heat stress is equally dangerous, especially with young joeys.

d.) Minimize Stress

Injured animals should be kept in a warm, quiet, and dark area. Make sure the kangaroo is not exposed to loud noises or sudden movements.

If the animal is a joey, place it in its pouch, and then put the pouch inside a box. For larger macropods, use a blanket to increase their sense of security and to keep them warm.

In general, kangaroos don't like change and are thus highly susceptible to becoming stressed. They become very accustomed to the known elements of their environment and become nervous and high-strung when something is "different."

For this reason, it's always important to determine if something in the environment is what's really stressing the kangaroo rather than an illness or injury. Sometimes

Chapter 7 – Kangaroo Health

making an environmental correction is the only "treatment" a roo really needs.

Chapter 8 – Roo Human Interest Stories

Although at the time of this writing, some of these stories are out of date, each illustrates the unique relationship that can develop between kangaroos and the people who love them.

As the last account in this section points out, kangaroos are not ideal pets unless you have the right setting for their care and husbandry, but they are definitely beguiling.

When handraised, roos become quite tame, and are openly affectionate with their humans. Anyone who loves animals will attest to the bonds that can form between and transcend the boundaries of species and human perception.

1.) Oklahoma Women Moves into the Zoo

In order to stay with her beloved kangaroo companion, Irwin, an Oklahoma woman left her home and moved into the zoo. It's a novel solution to a highly unusual problem, but one that proves the depth of the relationships that develop between humans and animals.

In 2011, Christine Carr found comfort from her depression in a companion that arguably needed her as much as she needed him. Irwin, a red kangaroo weighing 25 lbs. / 11.34 kg at the time, was partially paralyzed and faced the threat of euthanasia.

In Carr's care, however, Irwin recovered well, going on daily errands in a car seat wearing shirts and pants. He became his doting human "mother's" constant companion.

The two met when Carr began to volunteer at a local animal sanctuary as part of her treatment for depression. A few days after Carr began to volunteer, Irwin ran into a fence and fractured his neck.

The injury and resulting brain damage left him partially paralyzed. Carr convinced the staff to allow her to nurse the injured kangaroo back to health.

In 2011, when Carr and Irwin first began to attract media attention, the kangaroo couldn't stand or walk unassisted, but he was beginning to be able to hop. The connection between Carr and Irwin was intense. Everyone was happy with the arrangement, except worried local officials.

A fully grown red kangaroo will weigh more than 200 pounds / 91 kg and can stand up to 7 feet / 2.13 meters tall. When the animals are in full possession of their mobility, they can cover a distance of 25 feet / 7.62 meters in one jump.

Veterinarians did not believe that Irwin would ever grow that large however, guessing that at his heaviest, he would be no more than 50 lbs. / 23 kg. Carr wanted to keep Irwin with her at home.

Assurances that the kangaroo would remain small did not settle down the mayor and city council, however. Carr's therapist had Irwin certified as a therapy animal under the Americans with Disabilities Act, and still the "powers that be" fretted.

Meanwhile, the supposedly "dangerous" kangaroo became a favorite at the local nursing home, where elderly residents in wheelchairs cuddled and petted him.

Ultimately the city required Carr to take out a $50,000 / £30,583 liability insurance policy on Irwin. An anonymous donor paid for the insurance. Still, Carr fled to her parents' home in McAllister, Oklahoma, fearing that Irwin would be taken from her.

After two years of what became an harassing situation, the story had a happy ending. Carr and Irwin both moved to The Garold Wayne Interactive Zoological Park. The solution proved to be perfect for them both.

Carr loved working with all the animals and Irwin, although he couldn't interact with the park's other kangaroo due to his disability, immediately made friends with Larsen, a Siberian tiger cub.

The founder of the zoo, Joe Schreibvogel, gave a simple explanation for the arrangement, "We called her up and offered her a place to stay and Irwin a zoo to hang out with a bunch of other animals, and they've been here ever since."

2.) HOA Objects to Mike the Kangaroo

In Spring, Texas an overly-vigilant homeowners association cast sensitivity to the winds when it came to Mike, a 6-month-old red kangaroo serving as a therapy animal for a 16-year-old girl with Down's Syndrome.

The Estates of Legends Ranch Homeowners Association sent a letter to Nick and Jeni Dreis ordering them to get rid of their daughter Kayla's best friend.

"Please immediately remove the kangaroo from your property as it is not a household pet nor can it be maintained for business purposes," the letter declared.

That, however, was before local television stations got the word out and a global outcry was raised against the unfeeling HOA. Within days, a representative of the association was backpedaling.

"The letter should never have been sent," the representative said. "They (the HOA officials) were unaware that the kangaroo was being used for therapy purposes. We trust that the family is going to be working in good faith to find a more suitable home for the animal."

Nick and Jeni Dreis were indeed working in good faith, but not to meet the requirements of their bureaucratic HOA. The couple created a wildlife preserve, organic farm, and educational center in nearby Conroe for special needs children.

Mike, the kangaroo, who was still happily living in his pouch while all the fuss was going on, will be moved there when he grows larger.
The point of the center for the children is to learn life skills while interacting with animals that shower them with unconditional love and acceptance.

When a reporter asked Kayla how she would feel if her kangaroo had been taken away she said, "I would cry." Fortunately, that didn't happen and Mike remains her best friend and playmate.

3.) Queensland Man Advocates for Roo Lovers

Colin Candy has been fighting in court for 12 years since the Queensland Parks and Wildlife Service seized his red kangaroo, Mitchell. Candy found the joey on the side of the road near its dead mother and raised the baby by hand.

Candy has been through multiple appeals in his efforts to seek compensation from the government for Mitchell's seizure. He's taken the fight to the edge of bankruptcy, lost his wife, is estranged from his daughters, and battles depression.

The man sold his house to cover his expenses and now lives alone with five other hand-raised kangaroos.

His position is that because the red kangaroo is not a protected species, the animals do not fall under the jurisdiction of either state or federal law. His greater quest is not just to be compensated for all that he has lost since Mitchell was taken away, however. Candy has set his sights higher.

He wants the law to recognize the rights of people who raise native animals. Candy believes people should be able to keep kangaroos and other native species with a permit that acknowledges the animals have become domesticated.

Of his kangaroos, Candy told reporters, "They don't bark and annoy everyone and they don't chase the postman. People think I'm a nutter, but I hope one day everyone can have them."

Every year, Queensland undertakes the largest commercial harvesting of kangaroos in Australia, with 3.6 million killed for their hides and meat.

Candy decries the process as cruel and wrong, saying that if dogs or cats were treated in such a fashion, there would be public outrage.

"But if you do that to a kangaroo, it's OK," he said. "It's like they're a second-class citizen in their own country.

Although Candy admits he's lost every round in his long-standing legal battle, he insists he's winning the war because he continues to live his life with the kangaroos he loves.

4.) Kangaroo Rescue and Rehab in the U.S.

In 2002 Larry Rogers, an Instructor of Marketing at Ohio University, and his wife Tammy, were six years into running a kangaroo rescue and rehabilitation operation on their farm in Lancaster.

The founders of the now defunct International Kangaroo Society, the Rogers became kangaroo owners in 1997, struggling to learn how to care for the exotic animals.

Their first pet, a wallaby named Sidney, died of an hereditary condition. They spend years trying to find accurate health information only to discover that even exotic veterinarians in the United States had scant knowledge at best about kangaroos.

"The education aspect of kangaroo ownership is one that we have worked extremely hard to improve," said Rogers. In 2002, their farm was the only rescue and rehabilitation center for kangaroos in the nation.

Although Rogers expressed great affection for kangaroos, he was frank in his assessment that they do no make great pets. "They are difficult to keep and susceptible to a multitude of injuries and illnesses," he said.

"Because of these factors, we do not sell them. However, if someone proves that they are serious about obtaining one, we will work with them," Rogers continued.

Although cautionary about encouraging a proliferation of pet kangaroos, Tammie Rogers admitted that the joeys were her babies. "I take them everywhere - church, shopping, concerts, you name it," she said.

"When I tell women with children about the amount of time I spend with the baby kangaroos, they often say, 'Baby kangaroos sound like more work than newborns - how do you do it?'"

Both the Rogers said that kangaroos instantly captured their hearts and were a daily reminder of "how unique God's creation is."

Kid Talk: Understanding the Kangaroo's World

The one thing pretty much everyone knows about a kangaroo is that they raise their babies inside a pouch in the mother kangaroo's tummy.

The babies, called, joeys, ride around in there for several months, nursing on their mother's milk and growing big enough to start hopping in and out on their own.

A World of Marsupials

What you may not realize, however, is that kangaroos aren't the only animals with pouches. There are other "marsupials" around the world that raise their babies the same way. In Australia, there's a smaller version of the kangaroo called a wallaby.

Some people describe wallabies as "mini kangaroos," but they are completely different animals. They are, however, about half the size of a kangaroo, generally standing 3.5 feet tall and less (1.06 meters).

In fact, there are 334 different kinds of marsupials, including the American opossum, which actually looks a lot like a big rat with jagged teeth. They're just about the same the size as a large house cat.

"Possum" mothers have pouches, but the babies will also ride around clinging to her fur, which makes for a really funny sight. Because opossums don't see well in the daylight, they always look a little cross-eyed. They will hiss

Kid Talk: Understanding the Kangaroo's World

if they feel scared, but their real defense mechanism is to fall over and play "dead."

Kangaroos, The Biggest Marsupial

The kangaroo is the best known of all the marsupials because it's the biggest. There are images of kangaroos all over the place, and many people think they'd love to have one for a pet.

Unless you have a lot of room outdoors, that's not such a great idea though, since Red Kangaroos can grow to be 7 feet tall / 2.13 meters!

Kangaroos graze on grass and sometimes eat the leaves off of bushes and shrubs to live. Like cows, they basically digest their food twice. You'll see them working their jaws chewing their "cud" which only makes their kind of bored expression all the funnier.

Watch their ears. They can move them just like a cat, swiveling to pick up on nearby sounds. A kangaroo may look bored, but he knows exactly what's going on around him all the time!

Keep Your Distance from Wild Kangaroos

That very fact is why it's important not to just walk up to a kangaroo you encounter in the wild. You can't know how the kangaroo will react to you based on what it knows about humans already, or what you may be "saying" in kangaroo language without meaning to.

Kid Talk: Understanding the Kangaroo's World

Groups of kangaroos are called "mobs." One male kangaroo (called a buck, a boomer, or a jack) is in charge of the whole group, with the younger males letting him be the boss. The lead male will be the father of all the joeys born in the mob.

If you walk up to the lead male and look him right in the eye, he may think you're challenging his role as the leader. If you do that, the male will probably stand up really straight to look as big as possible, and he may even thump the ground with his tail.

Don't turn around and run! Kangaroos can move at 35 mph / 56 kph and they can kick you while they're doing it! Instead, you need to look down, back away slowly, and it wouldn't hurt to cough real low and deep in your throat. That will tell the "boss" kangaroo that you know he's boss!

Female kangaroos can get a little "touchy" to be around, too because they have babies to protect. Basically, it's just best to mind your manners around kangaroos you run into in the wild and let them be kangaroos.

In Australia, "roos" come into neighborhoods on the edge of town and people feed them. During dry, hot weather, it's okay to help out animals, but do it at a distance. Don't try to get a kangaroo "tame" enough to eat out of your hand.

It might be a lot of fun for you, but if the kangaroo then acts badly around someone else, then there's a problem about where he can live and be safe around people. Always think about how your actions might affect the animal.

Kid Talk: Understanding the Kangaroo's World

Big Kangaroos Start Out Really Small

It's hard to imagine that these animals that get so big and tall they could hurt you (usually without meaning to) start out life so small they're no bigger than a tiny bean!

Most baby animals grow inside their mothers until they're old enough to be born. This doesn't happen with kangaroos.

After about a month, the baby kangaroo or joey is born, but he doesn't have any hair, his eyes aren't open, and only his front legs work — which is good, because he needs them for what comes next.

The little baby takes an incredible three-minute journey to make his start in life. He crawls up his mother's body and into the pouch to find one of her nipples.

Once inside the pouch, where it's warm and dark, the little joey needs about 15 minutes to find the nipple, but then he latches on and stays there for about six months, eating, and getting bigger and bigger!

After six months, the little guy is ready to start jumping in and out of its mother's pouch. She may have to help him by bending down and leaning forward. He'll jump into her pouch head forward, turn a fast somersault, and then pop his head up to look around.

When it's time for the mother to have another baby, she has to stop the bigger joey from getting into her pouch.

Kid Talk: Understanding the Kangaroo's World

Sometimes, if he really isn't getting the idea, she just dumps him out on the ground!

For about four months after that, the mother will still let the joey nurse. He'll stay close to her even as he grows bigger and bigger. Sometimes all the male kangaroos in a mob hang out together, and the females and half-grown joeys have their own group as well.

Kid Talk: Understanding the Kangaroo's World

Hopping to Get Along

The other thing that everyone knows about kangaroos is that they hop rather than run. In fact, they're the only big animal that use hopping as their main way of moving.

What's interesting about how a kangaroo hops is that his speed and how far he can jump — sometimes more than 25 feet / 7.62 meters at a time — isn't because the muscles in his legs are strong.

If you could see where the muscles are attached to the kangaroo's leg bones, you'd be looking at really tough, strong cords called tendons. A kangaroo's tendons have the ability to store energy.

If you've ever played with a spring, imagine pressing the coils of the spring down as tight as you can and then letting go really fast. The spring bursts open from all the stored energy of having been pushed down or "compressed."

That's what happens with a kangaroo's tendons. Every time the roo lands on the ground while he's hopping, all the energy gets pushed down into the tendons. Then as the too comes up in the hop, all that force is released and pushes him forward.

The more times this happens, the more energy the kangaroo can store in his tendons. He doesn't have to work hard at all to hop, and the longer he hops, the farther he jumps each time.

Kid Talk: Understanding the Kangaroo's World

He's so good at this motion that scientists have found out the kangaroo is the most efficient animal on earth when he's hopping.

But he can only do that if he's moving forward. Kangaroos can't go backwards at all! They can, however, swim really well, which they'll do if they get really scared and can't find another way to escape.

Do They Box?

The idea that kangaroo's box like fighters with boxing gloves on is just a way to describe how kangaroos will rough house and sometimes fight with each other. Just look at how a kangaroo is built.
They have those big back legs, so they stand upright most of the time with their shorter front legs held loose like arms. If a roo is just moving around slowly in an area, he may hunch over and shuffle, but he really doesn't walk on all fours.

So, if two kangaroos are having a disagreement or just kind of wrestling, they face each other standing up and use their front legs to hit and swipe at one another. It really does look like boxing.

The one thing you really don't want is for a kangaroo to kick you. Their legs are really strong, and even a small roo can easily knock a man down.

Can They Be Tame?

Kid Talk: Understanding the Kangaroo's World

Kangaroos can be very tame if they are taken away from their mothers when they are young and bottle fed. All the bonding that would usually happen with the mother kangaroo is transferred to the humans.

Little joeys that are being bottle fed are kept in warm cloth pouches. The best way to make a little bottle-fed joey feel safe is to wear his pouch and take him with you all the time. No wonder he starts thinking about you as his best friend!

Kangaroos that are kept as pets are very loving and very loyal, but they can't be kept inside for more than about a year because they just get too big. If you live out in the country though, and have a nice, big, fenced area for a kangaroo, they can be wonderful pets and will live as long as 20 years.

Afterword

Especially in its native Australia, the kangaroo has an iconic image. It's easy to feel as if you're looking at roos everywhere! On signage, on the money, on the national coat of arms.

It doesn't matter that there are 334 species of marsupials in the world — the kangaroo is the best known and in many ways the most beloved.

Just look at a female — a jill — standing upright and looking back at the camera with that matter-of-fact expression complete with placid eyes and firmly set mouth.

Since kangaroos are cattle-like in their digestion, the jill staring back at you may be contemplatively chewing her cud.

Then, out of nowhere, a little head pops up out of the pouch and a joey gazes at you with the same mild-mannered look in miniature. You can't help it. You're hooked.

Keeping a kangaroo as a pet is not, however, the easiest of propositions as you hopefully now realize. In addition to discussing the ins and outs of husbandry throughout the text, I ended the book with several human interest stories.

The people profiled in the last chapter all exhibited great love for one or more kangaroos — and almost all found

Afterword

themselves at odds with the "authorities" in defense of their pets.

Part of the perceived problem with kangaroos kept domestically is their physical size. Some species can reach 7 feet (2.13 meters) and more, and then there's the bit about the "boxing."

Domesticated roos aren't typically aggressive, unless they're rough-housing with one another, but the image is there in the popular perception and thus very hard to eradicate.

The truth is that keeping a kangaroo is, for all practical purposes, a matter of having exotic "livestock." If you don't have land in a rural setting where you can build a proper enclosure with fencing, I strongly discourage you from the idea of having a roo for a pet.

If, however, your setting is right and there are no legal snarls, becoming a surrogate "parent" to a roo can be one of the most rewarding experiences you'll ever have with an animal. Certainly there are no pets quite like kangaroos.

At the very least, I hope I have left you with a new appreciation for these animals and for the extraordinary way they come into the world as neonates.

No matter how often I write about or am witness to images of the process, that tiny baby climbing up into the pouch always strikes me as the bravest of little souls.

Afterword

Regardless of where you stand on kangaroo ownership, I suspect you are already a kangaroo lover. There are many ways to support the conservation of these animals in the wild. In particular I commend to you the efforts of the World Wildlife Fund on behalf of rare and endangered tree kangaroos.

(See wwf.panda.org/what_we_do/endangered_species/tree_kangaroo/)

I still have no idea if Dr. Doolittle's wish to curse in kangaroo has any basis in reality, but I do know that kangaroos speak eloquently for themselves and their message is a fascinating one for we mere humans.

Frequently Asked Questions

Although I recommend that you read the entirety of the text to learn as much as you can about kangaroos and their care, the following are some of the most "frequently asked questions" that I encounter about these fascinating marsupials.

Do male kangaroos have pouches like the females?

No. There is no species of marsupial in which the males have a pouch or a marsupium. That's a distinctive feature of female kangaroos.

I've heard that some male kangaroos have two penises?

That's a misunderstanding of the term "bifurcated," meaning the male's penis has two tips. This is true in many species of wallabies, but it is not true in the large kangaroo species.

Then is it true that female kangaroos have multiple reproductive organs?

No, but a female kangaroo's reproductive system is highly specialized because their young do not develop in a placenta as is the case with most mammals.

Females have the ability to have one joey nursing in the pouch while a second embryo is more or less placed on "hold" until the first infant is weaned.
How long do kangaroos live?

Frequently Asked Questions

Lifespan varies slightly by species, but a well-cared-for captive kangaroo can live 20 years or more.

Do kangaroos make sounds?

For the most part, kangaroos are quiet animals. Males will growl at one another before they fight, and they make clucking noises at females during mating season.

How do kangaroos in the wild maintain their population?

Kangaroos are highly responsive to prevailing environmental conditions. Females can delay the development of their offspring for months through a process called diapause.

Australia is a very dry continent, so this ability is extremely useful to help kangaroos maintain their population and increase survival rates during periods of drought. The species can subsist for weeks with very little water, and so is naturally drought resistant.

This is not to suggest that roos don't starve or die of dehydration during bad times; they do. As a species, however, they are well adapted to take advantage of the most favorable conditions to maintain their population numbers.

This even extends to the ability in females to delay the birth of their joeys through a process called embryonic diapause.

Frequently Asked Questions

Do kangaroos make good pets?

Yes, they do, if you have the right circumstances to keep them. Hand-raised joeys grow into affectionate and loyal companions, but as adults, they need a spacious outdoor enclosure.

Is it hard to hand-raise a joey?

Joeys demand a lot of attention. They need you to serve as their surrogate "mother" and give them the sense of security they would normally derive from maturing in their mother's pouch.

When you're hand raising a joey, it's really best to just wear their substitute pouch. The more you can do this, the greater the chances the baby will thrive.

Obviously, this is a terrific bonding experience, and part of the reason kangaroos are known for being affectionate and loyal.

Do kangaroos get along with other pets and children?

In many cases, you really should ask if your existing pets will get along with the kangaroo. When you're asking animals of different species to interact, predicting what will happen can be tough.

Never leave your pets unsupervised. A young joey can be seriously injured by a family dog that is just playing too hard, but by the same token, an adult kangaroo can inflict terrible damage with a well-placed kick.

Frequently Asked Questions

You must not keep kangaroos with cats. Feline feces can contain the protozoan that causes toxoplasmosis. The condition is fatal to joeys.

Teach young children to interact with all animals with kindness and respect. A kangaroo joey has delicate bones and is subject to stress, especially at a young age. Children must be made to understand this.

Typically, pet kangaroos are not aggressive and they give clear signs if they are getting annoyed about something. The best recommendation is good supervision of all parties concerned until everyone knows how to behave themselves.

How much and how often should I feed my joey?

Since you will be giving a joey supplemental feed, you will need to follow the manufacturer's guidelines as laid out in the feeding and growth charts supplied as part of the standard packaging for these products.

Mother kangaroos vary the composition of their milk according to the nutritional needs of the joey at each developmental stage. Milk replacement products attempt to reproduce this process.
If you bought your joey from a breeder, that person should be able to give you solid advice on hand-rearing products and procedures.

Frequently Asked Questions

How do I "toilet" a joey?

In the wild, female kangaroos lick the joey's anal region to stimulate urination and defecation. Replicate this process by gently tapping or lightly stroking the area with a tissue or warm washcloth.

Toilet the joey after each feeding, and when it wakes up from a nap. Carry the baby to the toilet and hold it gently but securely over the bowl.

Give your pet adequate time to completely finish its "business." This may take a few minutes. Kangaroos spurt when they urinate rather than producing a steady stream.

Regularly toileting a joey is extremely important. Failure to do so can lead to urinary tract, kidney, and bowel disease.

Can kangaroos be housebroken?

No. Some people claim they've gotten joeys to use pads or papers in the house, but breeders say this is not possible. After the first few months, your roo is going to be too large to keep inside anyway, and must be moved to an outdoor enclosure.

Why are playpens good for joeys?
For the same reason they're good for human children. Kids get into trouble fast! A playpen will safely contain your pet when you can't supervise what the baby is up to. Don't underestimate just how curious a kangaroo can be!

A playpen allows the joey to hop in and out of its pouch at will, but to remain in a comfortable and safe area. This level of containment won't last long, but it's very useful for the time when it is effective.

(Note that when hanging a joey's pouch from the side of the playpen, the bottom of the pouch should not touch the floor of the pen.)

When should a joey be weaned?

Many breeders believe joeys should be allowed to take a bottle as long as they like. In time, the baby will get interested in solid food on its own, especially if you begin to offer it a few shoots of green grass.

When a joey becomes interested in solid food, what should I give it?

Start with a few shoots of green grass to get the joey used to the idea of chewing rather than suckling. Once he's doing that well, you can begin to transition to the adult foods discussed in Chapter 4.

Relevant Websites

San Diego Zoo
www.animals.sandiegozoo.org/animals/kangaroo-wallaby

National Geographic – Red Kangaroo
www.animals.nationalgeographic.com/animals/mammals/red-kangaroo

Australia Zoo
www.australiazoo.com.au/our-animals/amazing-animals/mammals/?mammal=kangaroos

Live Science
www.livescience.com/27400-kangaroos.html

Defenders of Wildlife
www.defenders.org/kangaroo/basic-facts

Kangaroo Facts
www.giftlog.com/pictures/kangaroo_facts.htm

Kangaroo Information for Kids
ww2.valdosta.edu/~mccrews/topic.html

The Kangaroo Trail
www.rootourism.com

Kangaroo Conservation Center
www.kangaroocenter.com

Queensland Government

Relevant Websites

Department of Environment and Heritage Protection
Kangaroos
www.ehp.qld.gov.au/wildlife/livingwith/kangaroos.html

Australia's Amazing Kangaroos and the Birth of Their Young
www.answersingenesis.org/articles/cm/v10/n4/australias-amazing-kangaroos

Australian Government
Department of Foreign Affairs and Trade
www.dfat.gov.au/facts/kangaroos.html

Arkive - Western Grey Kangaroo
www.arkive.org/western-grey-kangaroo/macropus-fuliginosus/

Arkive - Red Kangaroo
www.arkive.org/red-kangaroo/macropus-rufus/

National Geographic
Eastern Gray Kangaroo
animals.nationalgeographic.com/animals/mammals/gray-kangaroo/

National Geographic
Red Kangaroo
animals.nationalgeographic.com/animals/mammals/red-kangaroo

Melbourne Museum - Red Kangaroo

Relevant Websites

museumvictoria.com.au/melbournemuseum/discoverycentre/wild/victorian-environments/mallee/red-kangaroo/

Kangaroo Creek Farm
"Keeping and Breeding Kangaroos"
www.kangaroocreekfarm.com/id4.html

Glossary

buck – A common or colloquial term for a male kangaroo. Also called a boomer or a jack.

boomer – A common or colloquial term for a male kangaroo, also called a buck or a jack.

conception – The process by which sperm from a male joins with an ovum or egg from a female to create a developing fetus (baby) in the womb.

diapause - A reproductive capability present in some insects, invertebrates, and mammals. Diapause allows for the suspension of embryonic development due to unfavorable environmental conditions or, in the case of kangaroos, the presence of another offspring in a later stage of development in the marsupium or pouch.

doe – A common or colloquial term for a female kangaroo, also called a jill.

estrus cycle – A period of fertility in the female of any species that occurs at regular intervals during which eggs are produced and are ready for conception with sperm from a male.

gestation – The developmental period of time spent by a fetus in the womb of any species. In kangaroos, the lengthiest stage of development is not in the womb. A kangaroo fetus is not encased in a placenta, but is born as a

Glossary

neonate, which then climbs into the pouch to finish its development attached to one of the mother's teats.

herbivores – Any species of animal that relies on plants as its primary means of subsistence.

hybridization – The cross-breeding of two different species or subspecies either naturally or in captivity under controlled circumstances to produce a unique hybrid offspring.

jack – Common or colloquial term for a male kangaroo, also called a buck or a boomer.

jill - Common or colloquial term for a female kangaroo, also called a doe.

joey – Common or colloquial term for a baby kangaroo and for the offspring of all macropods.

kangaroo - The largest members of the family of marsupials called "macropods" short for *Macropodidae*.

macropod – An animal belonging to the family of marsupials. Macropods include kangaroos, wallaroos, wallabies, tree-kangaroos and pademelons. The literal translation of the term "macropod" is "large foot."

marsupial – A type of mammal that carries its young in a pouch or marsupium as it develops rather than in a placenta in the mother's womb.

Glossary

marsupium - The pouch of a female marsupial where the baby or joey finishes its development after emerging from the womb as a partially developed neonate. The amount of time a joey spends in the womb varies by species.

neonate - The partially developed young of a marsupial that emerges from the womb at birth to crawl into the mother's pouch or marsupium to complete its development attached to one of the mother's nipples.

pademelon - A species of forest-dwelling wallaby.

polygynous – A mating system in which males have more than one female partner.

portmanteau - A word form in which two sounds and meanings of different words are combined to create a new meaning as in "wallaby" and "kangaroo" to arrive at "wallaroo." Note that the term "wallaroo" is not used in Australia.

ruminant - Mammals that regurgitate their food as rumen, which they chew as "cud."

subspecies – Variations of the same species, generally classified by geographical location.

wallaby - A name used informally for about 30 species of macropods that are physically smaller than both kangaroos and wallaroos.

Glossary

wallaroo - A combination of the words "wallaby" and "kangaroo" to describe animals of an intermediate size in the macropod family. Note that this term is not used in Australia.

Index

Antilopine Kangaroo, 16, 19
appetite, 43
body temperature, 48, 69, 80, 82
bowel prolapse, 75
breeder, 37, 40, 41, 45, 49, 67, 110
breeding, 26, 40, 60, 118
cats, 37
commercial pellets, 52
cost, 37, 38, 39, 49
cow's milk, 46
Dangerous Wild Animals Act, 35
diarrhea, 43, 75, 76, 77
Eastern Grey Kangaroo, 16, 18, 19
embryonic diapause, 60, 108
eyes, 43
feeding, 1, 44, 46, 49, 50, 51, 52, 57, 77, 110, 111
Female, 60, 61
fencing, 54, 104
first aid, 80
fleas, 74, 75
food, 43, 57, 58
hair loss, 74
hayrack, 53
herbivores, 17, 23, 118

holding area, 55, 56
hopping, 16, 21, 93, 99, 100
illness, 43
injuries, 79
injury, 43, 80
intellectual stimulation, 57
joeys, 80
latches on, 60
lice, 74, 75
Lumpy Jaw, 77, 78
male, 18, 26, 61, 107, 117, 118
marsupial, 34
marsupials, 82
mate, 26, 61
monthly costs, 39
mouth, 43, 81
neonate, 2, 14, 59, 61, 62, 63, 65, 118, 119
nose, 43
nostrils, 63, 81
other pets, 44
pen, 43
playpen, 51, 111, 112
pneumonia, 77
pouches, 48, 68, 70, 93, 101, 107
probiotics, 76
purchase, 44
pyrethrum powders, 74
recreation, 57

Index

Red Kangaroo, 1, 15, 16, 17, 18, 42, 113
reproductive cycles, 60
solid foods, 51
space, 44
symptoms, 76, 77
Thrush, 76
ticks, 75
toxoplasmosis, 37
treatment, 77
water, 58
Western Grey Kangaroo, 16, 18
womb, 2, 14, 59, 60, 117, 118, 119